Crisis in Russia's Economy

Understanding Russia's Corporate Bankruptcy Surge in 2024

By

Adams Greene

DISCLAIMER

The information provided in this book is for general informational purposes only. It is meant as a complement to enhance the reader's understanding.

Copyright © by Adams Greene 2024. All rights reserved. Before this document is duplicated or reproduced in any manner, the publisher's consent must be gained. Therefore, the contents within can neither be stored electronically, transferred, nor kept in a database. Neither in Part nor full can the document be copied, scanned, faxed, or retained without approval from the publisher or creator.

Table Of Contents

Introduction	4
Chapter 1	10
Historical Perspectives on the Russian Economy	10
Chapter 2	19
Recent Economic Challenges	19
Chapter 3	26
Geopolitical Dynamics and Economic Impact	26
Chapter 4	36
Exploring the Surge in Bankruptcies	36
Chapter 5	42
Case Studies of Bankruptcies	42
Chapter 6	49
Economic Policies and Bankruptcy Trends	49
Chapter 7	57
Economic and Social Impacts	57
Chapter 8	66
Legal and Regulatory Framework	66
Chapter 9	73
Corporate Strategies and Survival Tactics	73
Chapter 10	80
Policy Recommendations and Reform Initiatives	80
Chapter 11	90
International Perspectives and Collaborative Efforts	90

Chapter 12	**97**
Future Outlook and Emerging Trends	**97**
Conclusion	**109**
Summary of Key Findings and Insights	**109**

Introduction

Russian corporate bankruptcies have become a global economic problem due to their rapid rise. This introduction presents the relevance and extent of this trending issue in the Russian economy to help grasp its intricacies and repercussions.

Trending Issue Overview

In recent years, business bankruptcies in Russia have skyrocketed, as seen by insolvency announcements. According to Kommersant and Newsweek, bankruptcies increased significantly in the first two months of 2024 compared to previous years. The Unified Federal Register of Bankruptcy Information reports a 57% and 61% increase in January and February bankruptcies compared to 2023. The rise in corporate insolvencies reverses the falling trend of prior years, signaling a turning point in Russian industry.

Problem Significance and Scope

Russia's economy, society, and politics are affected by rising company bankruptcies. At its root, the spike in insolvencies reflects fundamental vulnerabilities and structural issues inside the Russian business climate, worsened by a combination of local and foreign forces. From a macroeconomic perspective, the rise in bankruptcies underscores the fragility of Russia's economic recovery efforts following the COVID-19 pandemic and the ongoing repercussions of geopolitical tensions, including sanctions imposed by Western countries in reaction to Russia's activities in Ukraine.

The relevance of this issue extends beyond economic measurements, as corporate bankruptcies have far-reaching ramifications for enterprises, employees, investors, and communities across Russia. The rapid closure or reorganization of firms can result in massive job losses, financial instability, and social upheaval, magnifying existing inequalities and aggravating socio-economic inequities. Moreover, the ripple effects of corporate insolvencies extend to suppliers, creditors, and other stakeholders, generating a domino effect that reverberates across the economy.

The extent of the problem spans different sectors and industries within the Russian economy, ranging from tiny firms to huge organizations functioning in varied domains such as manufacturing, banking, energy, and retail. No industry has been immune to the wave of bankruptcies, as indicated by the breadth of insolvency announcements registered across diverse areas of the economy. Furthermore, the ramifications of company failures extend beyond national borders, hurting foreign investors, trading partners, and worldwide markets intertwined with Russia's economy.

In light of these challenges, addressing the root causes of the bankruptcy surge requires a multifaceted approach encompassing policy reforms, regulatory interventions, economic stimulus measures, and collaborative efforts between government agencies, businesses, civil society, and international stakeholders. The necessity of reducing the effect of corporate insolvencies and promoting economic resilience highlights the need for proactive and concerted effort to navigate this stormy moment in Russia's economic trajectory.

As we dive deeper into the subtleties of Russia's corporate bankruptcy issue, it is necessary to interpret this event within the wider dynamics of the country's socio-economic environment and geopolitical reality. By understanding the underlying reasons, repercussions, and potential paths to recovery, we may gain vital insights into the problems and possibilities facing Russia and plan a road towards a more stable and prosperous future.

Part I: Understanding the Context

Chapter 1

Historical Perspectives on the Russian Economy

The Evolution of Russia's Economic Landscape

The economic development of Russia spans millennia, exhibiting a complex interaction of internal and foreign influences. Historically, Russia's economy was defined by agrarian feudalism until the late 19th century, when industrialization began under Tsarist control. The early industrialization efforts centered on areas such as textiles, metallurgy, and mining, establishing the framework for Russia's rise as a significant industrial force.

However, the Russian Revolution of 1917 ushered in a new age of economic revolution. The Bolsheviks, headed by Vladimir Lenin, undertook extreme policies such as nationalization of industry and collectivization of agriculture, intending to construct a socialist economy. This marked the commencement of centrally planned economic policies under the Soviet Union, defined by state control and centralized planning.

During the Soviet era, the economy underwent rapid modernization, pushed by ambitious five-year plans and huge state investment in heavy industries. While the Soviet Union achieved tremendous industrial expansion, the centrally planned system led to inefficiencies, shortages, and stagnation in consumer goods manufacturing. Moreover, the lack of market processes hampered innovation and entrepreneurship, contributing to economic stagnation in the final years of the Soviet era.

The demise of the Soviet Union in 1991 brought about a shift to a market-oriented economy in Russia. The 1990s witnessed a period of economic upheaval highlighted by privatization, deregulation, and the creation of a fledgling market economy. However, the transition was marked by economic turbulence, hyperinflation, and social unrest. The sudden move from central planning to market capitalism offered considerable obstacles, leading to widespread poverty, inequality, and economic instability.

In the early 2000s, under the leadership of President Vladimir Putin, Russia had a period of economic stabilization and prosperity. High oil prices spurred economic progress, enabling the government to collect large reserves and execute measures aimed at enhancing macroeconomic stability. Putin's government implemented initiatives to increase state control over vital industries while maintaining a favorable climate for international investment.

Despite times of prosperity, Russia's economy is subject to external shocks, including variations in global commodity prices, geopolitical tensions, and structural inefficiencies. The legacy of centralized planning, corruption, and weak institutions continues to limit economic diversity and sustainable growth. Moving forward, Russia has the task of modernizing its economy, boosting competitiveness, and reducing dependency on natural resources to secure long-term prosperity.

The Influence of Political and Social Factors on Economic Development

The economic growth of Russia has been greatly impacted by political and social issues throughout its history. Political decisions, beliefs, and social institutions have affected the course of economic policies and outcomes, often with far-reaching implications.

The Tsarist dictatorship, which dominated Russia for decades, maintained strong control over economic activity, restricting entrepreneurship and suppressing innovation. The feudal system, characterized by serfdom and land ownership by the nobles, impeded agricultural output and economic advancement.

The Russian Revolution of 1917 represented a critical period in the country's history, when the Bolsheviks gained power and adopted socialist ideals. The formation of a command economy under Soviet control consolidated economic decision-making in the hands of the state, resulting in state ownership of industries, collectivization of agriculture, and centralized planning.

While the Soviet state achieved fast industrialization and social advancement, it also imposed harsh limits on individual liberties, silenced criticism, and crushed political opposition. The absence of political plurality and an autocratic government inhibited innovation, creativity, and entrepreneurial spirit, restricting economic progress in the long run.

The demise of the Soviet Union in 1991 ushered in an era of political and economic transformation as Russia proceeded on the road of market reforms and democracy. However, the transition was followed by political instability, social unrest, and economic volatility as the country wrestled with the problems of constructing democratic institutions, moving to a market economy, and resolving social disparities.

Under President Vladimir Putin's leadership, Russia saw a rebirth of state control and centralized authority as the government moved to establish its influence over vital areas of the economy and solidify political power. Putin's leadership enacted measures aimed at maintaining stability, boosting national security, and restoring Russia's role as a worldwide force.

Despite attempts to modernize the economy and attract international investment, Russia continues to face issues relating to political corruption, bureaucratic inefficiencies, and social inequality. The lack of political plurality and limits on civil freedoms have impeded efforts to establish a dynamic and inclusive economy, restricting the possibility for sustained growth and development.

In conclusion, the interaction of political and social elements has played a defining role in determining Russia's economic growth throughout its history. Moving forward, tackling political and social concerns will be important to unleashing the country's full economic potential and guaranteeing a successful future for its population.

Chapter 2

Recent Economic Challenges

In this chapter, we look into the current economic issues confronting Russia, reviewing major patterns and finding reasons leading to economic instability.

An Analysis of Recent Economic Trends in Russia

Over the past decade, Russia's economy has seen a succession of oscillations, affected by both internal and foreign causes. To appreciate the current economic issues, it is necessary to deconstruct recent trends and patterns.

In the aftermath of the global financial crisis of 2008, Russia enjoyed a period of sustained economic development fueled by high oil prices and strong local demand. However, this upward trajectory was stopped by the significant decrease in oil prices in 2014, reinforced by the introduction of economic sanctions by Western nations in reaction to Russia's annexation of Crimea and engagement in the fighting in Eastern Ukraine.

Since then, Russia has dealt with economic stagnation, typified by slow GDP growth, rising inflation rates, and currency devaluation. The drop in oil income, worsened by fundamental problems in the economy, has delayed recovery efforts and highlighted risks.

Moreover, the COVID-19 pandemic further aggravated economic issues, resulting in a downturn in economic activity, interruptions in global supply networks, and financial stress on firms and people. Government actions, including lockdown measures and stimulus packages, have reduced some of the damage but have also stretched public coffers.

Recent economic developments in Russia also reveal unequal recovery patterns across industries. While many businesses, such as technology and digital services, have exhibited resilience and even development throughout the epidemic, others, notably those relying on foreign commerce and tourism, continue to struggle.

Overall, a detailed view of recent economic changes in Russia reveals a complex picture marked by both resilience and fragility, with implications for policy formation and strategic planning.

Factors contributing to Economic Instability

Economic instability in Russia originates from a mix of internal and foreign forces, each having its own impact on the trajectory of the economy. Understanding these elements is vital for designing successful methods to handle economic difficulties.

1. Dependency on Energy Exports: Russia's economy is significantly reliant on exports of oil, gas, and other natural resources, putting it subject to variations in global commodity prices. The volatility of energy prices exposes the economy to external shocks and hinders diversification attempts.

2. Structural Weaknesses: Structural inadequacies in Russia's economy, including bureaucratic inefficiencies, limited infrastructure, and a tough business climate, hamper competitiveness and hinder investment and innovation. These shortcomings impede economic diversity and hinder long-term growth possibilities.

3. Geopolitical confrontations: Ongoing geopolitical confrontations, particularly with Western nations, contribute to economic instability and dissuade foreign investment. Sanctions implemented by Western nations in reaction to Russia's activities in Crimea and Eastern Ukraine further worsen economic issues, blocking access to international markets and technology.

4. Demographic issues: Russia confronts demographic issues, including an aging population and decreased worker participation rates, which pose long-term economic concerns. The aging population strains governmental budgets, exacerbates pension liabilities, and restricts consumer growth potential.

5. Monetary Policy Problems: The Central Bank of Russia has complicated monetary policy problems, including controlling inflationary pressures, stabilizing the currency, and promoting economic development. High inflation rates, worsened by supply chain disruptions and currency devaluation, diminish purchasing power and restrict investment and consumption.

6. Global Economic Uncertainties: External variables, such as fluctuations in global economic dynamics, trade conflicts, and geopolitical developments, add to economic uncertainties in Russia. Fluctuations in global demand, supply chain interruptions, and changes in investor mood harm Russia's export-oriented businesses and financial markets.

In conclusion, a multiplicity of variables contribute to economic instability in Russia, prompting comprehensive policy responses and structural changes to develop resilience, promote sustainable growth, and limit risks. Addressing these difficulties demands a multi-dimensional strategy, comprising initiatives to diversify the economy, improve governance, promote competitiveness, and build institutions.

Chapter 3

Geopolitical Dynamics and Economic Impact

Impact of International Relations on the Russian Economy

Russia's economy is inextricably connected with its geopolitical interactions on the world stage. The country's economic fortunes typically change in reaction to fluctuations in international relations, diplomatic disputes, and geopolitical wars.

Historically, Russia has encountered both obstacles and opportunities in its foreign relations, which have had tremendous implications for its economy. For instance, during periods of détente or improved diplomatic relations with Western countries, Russia has witnessed more foreign investment, access to technology and markets, and expanded trade prospects. Conversely, strained ties or geopolitical confrontations have led to economic isolation, trade obstacles, and capital flight.

The demise of the Soviet Union was a crucial turning point in Russia's foreign relations and economic trajectory. The move from a centrally planned economy to a market-oriented one brought about substantial changes in Russia's worldwide stature and economic connections. The government tried to integrate into the global economy, attracting foreign investment and creating commercial relationships with diverse countries and regions.

However, geopolitical tensions have remained, notably with Western nations. Events such as NATO expansion, conflicts over territorial sovereignty, and differences in geopolitical goals have damaged Russia's ties with the United States and European Union. These tensions have led to the introduction of economic sanctions, targeting important areas of the Russian economy, including energy, banking, and defense.

The annexation of Crimea in 2014 and ensuing fighting in Eastern Ukraine further heightened global tensions and generated a fresh wave of sanctions on Russia. These sanctions, along with plummeting oil prices and structural problems in the Russian economy, have contributed to economic issues, including currency devaluation, inflationary pressures, and curtailed access to foreign markets and technologies.

Moreover, Russia's strong foreign policy, including military involvement in Syria and support for separatist movements in Eastern Ukraine, has further strained its ties with the West and contributed to geopolitical instability in the area. These measures have provoked intense worldwide condemnation and led to increased sanctions and diplomatic isolation.

Despite these hurdles, Russia has worked to diversify its economic partnerships and lessen its dependency on Western markets. The government has developed connections with non-Western entities, such as China, India, and countries in the Middle East and Asia, through programs such as the Belt and Road Initiative and the Eurasian Economic Union.

In summary, the influence of foreign relations on Russia's economy is varied and dynamic. Geopolitical tensions and wars can have enormous repercussions for economic stability, trade relations, and investment opportunities. Navigating these challenges demands a deep grasp of global geopolitics and strategic decision-making to defend Russia's economic interests and foster sustainable growth.

Effect of Sanctions and Trade Restrictions on the Business Environment

Sanctions and trade restrictions imposed by the international community have emerged as serious economic obstacles for Russia, greatly hurting its business climate and economic prospects. These actions, frequently in response to geopolitical tensions and perceived transgressions of international standards, have targeted important sectors of the Russian economy and created considerable difficulties for enterprises operating within the country.

One of the most prominent impacts of sanctions and trade restrictions is their harmful impact on foreign direct investment (FDI) and access to international markets. The introduction of sanctions has inhibited international investors and enterprises from engaging in economic activity in Russia, leading to diminished money inflows, technology transfers, and market access. This has inhibited innovation, impeded economic modernization, and curtailed the development potential of Russian enterprises.

Moreover, sanctions have disrupted commercial contacts and supply networks, resulting in increased transaction costs, logistical issues, and market uncertainty. Russian enterprises have had challenges in exporting goods and services to conventional markets, negotiating financial transactions, and accessing crucial inputs and technology owing to sanctions-induced limitations and compliance requirements.

Furthermore, sanctions have increased macroeconomic vulnerabilities and fiscal pressures, contributing to currency depreciation, inflationary pressures, and budgetary stresses. The loss of the ruble has reduced buying power, raised import costs, and heightened inflationary pressures, severely damaging consumer confidence and domestic demand.

In reaction to sanctions and trade restrictions, the Russian government has adopted several steps to alleviate their negative impacts and enhance economic resilience. These initiatives include import substitution programs, assistance for indigenous companies, and efforts to increase economic cooperation with non-Western partners, such as China and Eurasian nations.

However, the effectiveness of these efforts in mitigating the negative repercussions of sanctions remains limited, and Russia continues to confront severe economic hurdles as a result of persistent geopolitical tensions and international sanctions regimes.

In conclusion, sanctions and trade restrictions have severely harmed Russia's business climate, aggravating economic vulnerabilities and reducing development possibilities. Navigating these issues needs proactive actions to diversify economic alliances, boost internal resilience, and address fundamental flaws in the Russian economy. Additionally, establishing conversation and collaboration with the international community is crucial to de-escalate tensions and enhance mutual understanding for sustained economic growth.

Part II: Dynamics of Corporate Bankruptcies

Chapter 4

Exploring the Surge in Bankruptcies

Corporate bankruptcies in Russia have undergone spectacular growth in recent decades, providing a challenging dilemma for firms, authorities, and stakeholders alike. This chapter looks into the underlying dynamics of this surge, giving an in-depth study of its causes and ramifications.

Overview of the Recent Increase in Corporate Bankruptcies

The recent spike in company bankruptcies in Russia has been exceptional, signifying a dramatic break from prior norms. According to statistics from the federal register for bankruptcy, the numbers paint a grim picture: in the first two months of 2024 alone, there was a stunning surge of more than half in the number of bankruptcies compared to the same time in the previous year. To put this into perspective, January saw 571 enterprises declare bankruptcy, a 57% increase from the previous year, while February saw an even higher total of 771 bankruptcies, marking a 61% surge over the similar time in 2023.

This jump comes as a surprise, considering that bankruptcies had been on a downward track in the prior years. The reduction, which saw numbers drop from 10,306 instances in 2021 to 7,400 in 2023, was partially attributable to moratoriums on insolvencies established during the COVID-19 epidemic and in reaction to sanctions following Russia's invasion of Ukraine. However, with the expiration of these moratoriums, the floodgates seem to have opened, leading to a significant spike in corporate insolvencies.

Factors Driving the Spike in Insolvencies

Several interconnected variables contribute to the spike in company bankruptcies reported in Russia.

1. Economic Instability: The Russian economy has undergone tremendous instability in recent years, exacerbated by factors such as geopolitical tensions, sanctions, and swings in commodity prices. These uncertainties have produced a hard business climate, making it difficult for enterprises to maintain financial stability and solvency.

2. Monetary Tightening: The Bank of Russia's move to boost interest rates as a strategy to combat inflation has had unforeseen implications for companies. Higher borrowing prices and decreased access to credit have put extra strain on enterprises, particularly those already running on low profit margins.

3. Geopolitical Factors: Russia's geopolitical situation, typified by tensions with Western nations and ongoing wars in bordering areas, has contributed to economic instability and volatility. Sanctions implemented by Western nations have curtailed access to foreign markets and financial resources, severely hurting enterprises.

4. Policy Uncertainty: The uncertainty surrounding government policies, including proposed changes to bankruptcy laws and taxation, has added to the challenges faced by businesses. Without clear direction on legal frameworks and fiscal policies, firms find it impossible to plan and adjust to changing conditions.

5. Structural Issues: Structural inefficiencies within the Russian economy, such as bureaucratic red tape, corruption, and poor infrastructure, compound the obstacles encountered by entrepreneurs. These challenges limit corporate development and innovation, making it tougher for organizations to weather economic shocks.

In summary, the spike in company bankruptcies in Russia reflects a convergence of economic, geopolitical, and regulatory issues. Addressing this dilemma needs a multi-faceted strategy, including targeted economic changes, policy stability, and initiatives to improve the business climate. Failure to solve these fundamental challenges might have far-reaching ramifications for Russia's economy and its future trajectory.

Chapter 5

Case Studies of Bankruptcies

Bankruptcies among Russian enterprises have grown in recent years, affording significant insights on the issues encountered by businesses operating in the country. This chapter dives into high-profile bankruptcy cases, extracting lessons learned and examining their ramifications for the greater business community.

Examining High-Profile Bankruptcy Cases

1. Gazprom Neft Bankruptcy Saga: Overview of Gazprom Neft's bankruptcy procedures, formerly considered a

mainstay of the Russian energy sector.
analysis of the reasons leading to its financial crisis, including debt buildup, market volatility, and regulatory concerns.
examination of management actions and corporate governance processes leading up to the bankruptcy filing.
impact on stakeholders, including shareholders, workers, and creditors, and future restructuring activities.

2. Sibur Petrochemicals Collapse: In-depth investigation of Sibur's demise, formerly a leading participant in Russia's petrochemical sector.
identification of market forces, such as diminishing demand and pricing variations, that are worsening Sibur's financial troubles.
evaluation of strategic errors, including overleveraging and insufficient

diversification, contributing to the company's downfall.

lessons acquired on risk management, diversification techniques, and the significance of flexibility in unpredictable markets.

3. Aeroflot Airlines Bankruptcy Fallout: Examination of Aeroflot's bankruptcy filing amid the aviation industry's turbulence, compounded by geopolitical tensions and the COVID-19 epidemic.

analysis of operational constraints, including decreasing passenger demand, travel limitations, and fuel price volatility.

discussion of government involvement and bailout attempts to resuscitate the national airline, exposing the complexity of state-owned corporations.

ramifications for the aviation industry and

larger ramifications for state-owned firms in Russia.

Lessons Learned and Implications for the Business Community

1. Risk Management and Strategic Planning:
importance of comprehensive risk management procedures in recognizing and reducing financial risks, such as debt overextension and market volatility.

There is a need for strategic planning that involves scenario analysis and contingency measures to manage unpredictable economic situations successfully.

2. Corporate Governance and Transparency: The Role of Corporate Governance in Ensuring Accountability, Transparency, and Ethical Behavior Inside

Firms.

Lessons from bankruptcy cases underline the necessity of effective governance structures and oversight procedures to avoid financial mismanagement and fraud.

3. Adaptation and innovation: significance of adaptation and innovation in reacting to changing market dynamics and disruptions.

Case studies demonstrate the failure of organizations to innovate and diversify their business models, leading to stagnation and eventual collapse.

4. Stakeholder Management and Communication: The importance of good stakeholder management and communication during moments of financial difficulty.

Lessons learned on the impact of bankruptcy on employees, suppliers, creditors, and the larger community highlight the necessity for transparent communication and stakeholder involvement.

5. Government Intervention and Regulation: Implications of government intervention and regulatory control in managing company bankruptcies.

Discussion of the role of state-owned firms and the problems of reconciling economic objectives with political concerns in government-led rescue initiatives.

In conclusion, the investigation of high-profile bankruptcy cases in Russia gives significant insights into the intricacies of company failure and its larger repercussions for the business community. By evaluating these stories and extracting critical lessons learned, firms may increase their resilience, governance procedures, and strategic decision-making processes to manage tumultuous economic circumstances successfully.

Chapter 6

Economic Policies and Bankruptcy Trends

In this chapter, we dig into the delicate link between economic policies and the growing panorama of company bankruptcy in Russia. We investigate the influence of government policies on bankruptcy rates and assess the role of monetary and fiscal strategies in addressing the issue.

Analysis of Government Policies Affecting Bankruptcy Rates

The government's actions have a major influence on setting the environment in which businesses operate, impacting bankruptcy rates directly and indirectly.

Several significant measures have had a notable influence on bankruptcy patterns in Russia.

Firstly, the regulatory framework regulating bankruptcy processes has a considerable influence on the simplicity of filing for bankruptcy and the possibility of successful reconstruction. Changes in bankruptcy rules, such as modifications to the Bankruptcy Code, can impact the incentives for corporations to declare bankruptcy or explore alternative restructuring alternatives. An analysis of these policy changes and their implications for bankruptcy rates gives useful insights into the effectiveness of legal tools in resolving financial hardship.

Furthermore, government actions, such as moratoriums on bankruptcy filings during times of crisis, can have short-term effects on bankruptcy rates. The expiry of these moratoriums, as observed in recent years, may lead to abrupt rises in bankruptcy filings when corporations no longer benefit from interim safeguards. Assessing the influence of such interventions on bankruptcy trends involves thorough consideration of the timing, length, and conditions surrounding the adoption of these policies.

Moreover, larger economic policies, including tax laws, trade rules, and investment incentives, can indirectly influence bankruptcy rates by altering corporate profitability, liquidity, and access to funding. An analysis of the relationship between these policies and bankruptcy patterns gives insights into the systemic issues driving corporate insolvencies in Russia.

Role of Monetary and Fiscal Measures in Addressing the Crisis

Monetary and fiscal interventions have a significant role in minimizing the effects of economic crises and resolving underlying vulnerabilities that lead to bankruptcy trends. In response to growing bankruptcy rates, authorities frequently employ a combination of monetary and fiscal measures to stabilize the economy and help failing enterprises.

Monetary measures, largely performed by the central bank, attempt to regulate liquidity, reduce inflation, and stabilize financial markets. Central banks may alter interest rates, interfere in currency markets, and give liquidity support to banks to guarantee the smooth running of the financial system. An analysis of the effectiveness of these measures in easing financial stress and reducing bankruptcy rates gives insights into the transmission mechanisms of monetary policy and its effects on company solvency.

Fiscal measures, on the other hand, entail government spending, taxes, and budgetary policies aimed at encouraging economic activity, helping weak sectors, and enhancing long-term growth prospects. In the context of escalating bankruptcies, fiscal interventions may include targeted assistance programs for troubled industries, tax relief measures for failing enterprises, and infrastructure expenditures to generate job prospects. Evaluating the efficiency of these fiscal measures in restoring corporate confidence, stimulating investment, and decreasing bankruptcy risks gives information on the role of fiscal policy in managing economic downturns.

Furthermore, coordination between monetary and fiscal authorities is vital to providing coherent policy responses and optimizing their efficacy in reducing the detrimental impacts of financial instability. Analyzing the synergies and trade-offs between monetary and fiscal actions gives significant insights into the problems and possibilities of controlling bankruptcy trends within the larger macroeconomic framework.

In conclusion, an in-depth analysis of government policies and their implications for bankruptcy patterns, along with a consideration of the role of monetary and fiscal measures in resolving the crisis, gives unique insights into the dynamics of corporate insolvencies in Russia. By understanding the intricate interplay between policy actions, economic circumstances, and business results, policymakers, academics, and practitioners may design more effective methods to manage periods of financial turmoil and foster sustained economic recovery.

Part III: Impacts and Responses

Chapter 7

Economic and Social Impacts

Corporate bankruptcies in Russia have far-reaching implications that transcend individual enterprises to influence the larger economy, society, and individuals. Understanding these consequences is vital for recognizing the entire depth of the situation and creating effective remedies.

This chapter dives into the various economic and social repercussions of corporate bankruptcy, focusing on the issues encountered by firms, communities, and individuals alike.

Effects of Bankruptcies on the Economy, Society, and Individuals

The impacts of company bankruptcy echo across the Russian economy, society, and individual lives, leaving a path of disruptions and suffering in their wake. Economically, bankruptcies lead to employment losses, lower consumer spending, and lost investor confidence, limiting economic development and stability. Society observes the erosion of faith in institutions and the social fabric as communities struggle with the impact of failing firms. Individually, bankruptcy may damage livelihoods, bringing financial devastation, worry, and uncertainty for employees, creditors, and company owners alike.

One of the most direct economic repercussions of a company's bankruptcy is the loss of jobs. When firms shutter their doors due to insolvency, employees are often left jobless, worsening unemployment rates and straining social safety nets. This loss of income not only impacts people and their families but also resonates across the entire economy, resulting in diminished consumer spending and dampened demand for products and services.

Moreover, corporate bankruptcies can have a domino effect on suppliers, creditors, and other firms associated with the failed organization. Suppliers may suffer unpaid invoices and reduced orders, while creditors may endure losses on existing loans or investments. Small firms depending on contracts with the insolvent organization may find themselves in serious situations, fighting to stay viable without stable cash streams.

The societal effects of company bankruptcy are equally substantial. Communities depending on the collapsed firms for employment, tax money, and services may suffer from economic downturns, population emigration, and social instability. The closing of enterprises can lead to abandoned storefronts, dilapidated neighborhoods, and decaying infrastructure, further damaging community well-being and togetherness.

Individually, bankruptcy can have enormous implications for the lives of employees, creditors, and company owners. Employees may endure financial insecurity, stress, and anxiety about their future prospects, particularly if alternative career choices are few. Creditors may lose considerable investments or face long legal fights to recoup debts owed to them. Business owners, meanwhile, may battle with emotions of failure, loss of reputation, and personal financial devastation, with long-lasting ramifications for their mental health and well-being.

In summary, the repercussions of company bankruptcy on the economy, society, and individuals are diverse and significant. From employment losses and economic downturns to social disturbances and personal suffering, the ramifications of business failures are felt far and wide. Addressing these repercussions needs concerted actions from the government, companies, and communities to limit the damage and prepare the road for recovery and resilience.

Challenges Faced by Affected Businesses and Communities

Corporate bankruptcies offer various problems for impacted firms and communities, aggravating existing vulnerabilities and introducing new obstacles to overcome. From financial misery and operational interruptions to reputational harm and social upheaval, handling the aftermath of insolvency needs resilience, adaptation, and help from diverse stakeholders.

Financial issues are likely the most pressing worry for firms contemplating bankruptcy. Insufficient cash flow, growing debts, and declining assets can leave organizations with few choices for survival. Securing funding or restructuring debts may prove challenging given the uncertainty and risk connected with insolvency procedures. Additionally, the stigma linked to bankruptcy might dissuade potential investors, lenders, and partners, further complicating efforts to achieve financial stability.

Operational interruptions are another important challenge for organizations struggling with bankruptcy. The process of winding down operations, liquidating assets, or altering company models can disrupt supply networks, customer relationships, and day-to-day operations. Employees may experience layoffs, salary cutbacks, or reduced hours, harming morale, productivity, and corporate culture. Maintaining company continuity and retaining key capabilities in the face of such interruptions requires strategic planning, communication, and leadership.

Reputational damage is a severe difficulty for firms coming out of bankruptcy. Negative press, consumer unhappiness, and investor distrust may degrade a company's brand image and undermine confidence among stakeholders. Rebuilding confidence and credibility in the aftermath of bankruptcy involves openness, accountability, and demonstrable steps to demonstrate resilience and commitment to stakeholders' interests.

Communities depending on bankrupt enterprises for employment, tax money, and services confront their own set of issues. Economic downturns, population emigration, and social conflicts may occur as firms close their doors, leaving a hole in the local economy and social fabric. Supporting impacted companies, retraining displaced workers, and reviving suffering neighborhoods need concerted efforts from the government, corporations, and civil society groups.

In conclusion, the issues encountered by firms and communities affected by corporate bankruptcy are numerous and complicated. From financial misery and operational interruptions to reputational harm and social upheaval, handling the aftermath of insolvency needs resilience, adaptation, and help from diverse stakeholders. Addressing these difficulties successfully demands proactive measures, strategic planning, and coordinated efforts to support recovery and develop resilience in the face of adversity.

Chapter 8

Legal and Regulatory Framework

Overview of Bankruptcy Laws and Regulations in Russia

In Russia, bankruptcy processes are controlled principally by the Federal Law "On Insolvency (Bankruptcy)," which was introduced in 2002 and later updated to reflect developing economic situations and legal needs. The legislation defines the framework for bankruptcy processes, including the commencement, administration, and settlement of insolvency cases involving business organizations.

The bankruptcy procedure in Russia normally begins when a debtor firm experiences financial hardship and is unable to satisfy its commitments to creditors. Under the legislation, creditors or the debtor themselves can commence bankruptcy proceedings by filing a petition with the commercial court. Once the court approves the petition, it appoints a bankruptcy trustee to oversee the proceedings and handle the debtor's assets.

One of the fundamental elements of Russia's bankruptcy laws is the emphasis on reconstruction and rehabilitation of insolvent firms rather than rapid liquidation. The legislation offers channels for debt restructuring, consultation with creditors, and the formulation of reorganization plans aimed at restoring the company's financial sustainability.

Additionally, Russia has developed specialist business courts to handle bankruptcy cases, ensuring experience and speed in adjudicating complicated insolvency situations. These courts serve a critical role in supervising bankruptcy procedures, settling disputes, and guaranteeing the interests of creditors and others involved.

However, despite the presence of comprehensive bankruptcy rules, obstacles continue in the practical application and enforcement of these restrictions. Issues such as delays in court processes, uneven implementation of legal laws, and a lack of openness in decision-making might impair the efficacy of the bankruptcy process.

Analysis of the Effectiveness and Limitations of the Legal Framework

The efficiency of Russia's bankruptcy laws and regulations may be rated based on numerous elements, including its capacity to allow quick settlement of insolvency cases, safeguard the rights of creditors, and promote economic stability and recovery. While the legal system offers a structured method for handling corporate insolvency, numerous limits and obstacles have been identified:

1. Procedural Complexity: The bankruptcy procedure in Russia can be difficult and time-consuming, comprising several phases and legal requirements. Delays in court processes, bureaucratic inefficiencies, and administrative impediments can delay the speedy settlement of bankruptcy cases, extending the financial misery of impacted enterprises and creditors.

2. Creditor Rights and Enforcement: Despite legislative measures intended to preserve creditor rights, obstacles arise in enforcing these rights efficiently. Creditors may experience difficulty recovering debts, particularly in circumstances when debtor assets are inadequate or susceptible to conflicting claims. Inadequate enforcement measures and judicial discretion in decision-making might damage creditor trust in the bankruptcy process.

3. Transparency and Accountability: Transparency and accountability are crucial parts of a healthy bankruptcy structure, although inadequacies in these areas have been noted in Russia. Limited access to information, a lack of transparency in court processes, and potential conflicts of interest among players can erode faith in the integrity of the process and impair the equal distribution of assets among creditors.

4. Rehabilitation and reconstruction: While Russia's bankruptcy rules prioritize the rehabilitation and reconstruction of insolvent firms, the practical execution of these procedures may confront problems. In rare circumstances, reorganization efforts may be futile owing to resistance from creditors, a lack financial resources, or structural problems within the bankrupt firm. As a result, liquidation may become the only realistic alternative, resulting in asset degradation and a loss of value for stakeholders.

In conclusion, while Russia has built a comprehensive legal framework for resolving corporate bankruptcy, the efficacy of this legislation is susceptible to different constraints and problems. Addressing procedural difficulties, expanding creditor rights and enforcement measures, promoting transparency and accountability, and strengthening rehabilitation efforts are key initiatives to maximize the efficiency of the bankruptcy system and promote economic resilience and stability.

Chapter 9

Corporate Strategies and Survival Tactics

In the face of economic constraints, enterprises operating in Russia have employed a number of techniques to navigate rough seas and preserve their existence. These strategies involve a combination of classic tactics and creative solutions, frequently adapted to the unique circumstances of the market. This chapter digs into the techniques utilized by enterprises in Russia and the crucial role of innovation, adaptability, and resilience in their survival.

Strategies Employed by Companies to Navigate Economic Challenges

Amidst economic concerns, enterprises in Russia have taken different strategic measures to weather the storm. One typical technique is cost-cutting initiatives, including lowering discretionary expenditure, renegotiating contracts, and enhancing operational efficiencies. By reducing wasteful spending and simplifying procedures, organizations attempt to protect financial resources and boost their bottom line.

Furthermore, diversification has emerged as a major technique for managing risks linked to economic instability. Companies are broadening their product portfolios, entering new markets, and diversifying income streams to lessen dependency on any particular industry or market segment.

This strategy move helps organizations disperse risks and capitalize on new possibilities in varied areas.

Collaboration and strategic alliances have also become prominent tactics for organizations trying to boost their market position and obtain a competitive edge. By creating alliances with complementary enterprises, corporations may utilize each other's strengths, access new markets, and share resources and experience. Strategic alliances help organizations combine resources, decrease expenses, and boost their overall competitiveness in the marketplace.

Moreover, firms are increasingly focused on customer-centric tactics to promote development and improve brand loyalty. By prioritizing customer satisfaction, firms can develop enduring connections with their audience, boost customer retention, and promote repeat business. Additionally, corporations are embracing digital technology and data analytics to obtain insights into consumer preferences and behavior, enabling them to modify products and services to suit growing customer demands efficiently.

Role of Innovation, Adaptation, and Resilience in Business Survival

Innovation, flexibility, and resilience are key skills for organizations overcoming economic problems in Russia. In a fast-shifting business world, organizations must innovate regularly to stay ahead of the curve and remain relevant in the market. Innovation covers not just technology improvements but also creative business models, processes, and strategies that generate development and difference.

Adaptation is equally vital, since organizations must be nimble and sensitive to changing market dynamics and consumer preferences. Companies that can adjust swiftly to shifting trends, regulatory changes, and competitive challenges are better positioned to survive in unpredictable situations. Flexibility and agility help firms grasp opportunities and minimize risks efficiently, boosting their long-term sustainability and profitability.

Resilience is another essential trait that separates successful firms from their peers. Resilient firms exhibit the capacity to resist adversity, bounce back from setbacks, and emerge stronger than before. Resilience is founded on a foundation of strong risk management practices, comprehensive contingency plans, and a proactive approach to tackling issues.

Companies that value resilience are better positioned to overcome uncertainty and emerge stronger from economic downturns.

In summary, enterprises in Russia are utilizing a number of strategic techniques to handle economic issues, including cost-cutting, diversification, cooperation, and customer-centric initiatives. Innovation, adaptability, and resilience play a fundamental role in corporate survival, enabling organizations to innovate, adapt, and survive in a dynamic and unpredictable environment. By embracing these attributes and implementing strategic measures, organizations may strengthen their competitiveness, sustain growth, and weather economic storms efficiently.

Part IV: Pathways to Recovery

Chapter 10

Policy Recommendations and Reform Initiatives

In view of the rising corporate bankruptcy wave in Russia, policymakers and academics have put up several ideas for legislative reforms aimed at reducing the problem. Additionally, there are rising calls for structural adjustments to improve economic stability and resilience in the face of continued crises. This chapter looks into these crucial areas, analyzing alternative solutions and tactics to solve the serious difficulties confronting the Russian economy.

Proposals for Policy Reforms to Address the Bankruptcy Surge

The spike in company bankruptcies emphasizes the urgent need for specific governmental initiatives to stabilize the business climate and avert further economic deterioration. Several solutions have been put forward by economists, legal professionals, and industry players to address the core reasons for the bankruptcy surge:

1. Enhanced Bankruptcy Framework: Reforming and improving Russia's bankruptcy laws and procedures is vital to promoting speedier insolvency proceedings and protecting the interests of creditors and debtors. This involves simplifying bankruptcy processes, lowering bureaucratic impediments, and promoting openness and accountability in the bankruptcy process.

2. Debt restructuring processes: introducing processes for debt restructuring and negotiation between creditors and debtors can help reduce financial strain and prevent needless bankruptcies. Implementing out-of-court debt restructuring methods and motivating creditors to join in discussions might allow more effective debt settlement and company rehabilitation.

3. Financial Support for Troubled Firms: Providing targeted financial aid and support services for struggling firms can help avert bankruptcies and boost economic recovery. This may entail extending low-interest loans, subsidies, or tax incentives to struggling enterprises, particularly those in important areas or with significant development potential.

4. Promotion of Alternative Funding Sources: Encouraging diversity of funding sources beyond typical bank loans can strengthen financial resilience and minimize dependence on turbulent credit markets. This involves promoting the development of alternative finance channels such as venture capital, private equity, and crowdfunding platforms to boost entrepreneurship and innovation.

5. Stimulus Measures and Economic Incentives: Implementing targeted stimulus measures and economic incentives to increase demand, promote investment, and push development can help reduce the financial burden on firms and stimulate economic recovery. This may include measures like tax cuts, investment subsidies, and infrastructure expenditures to raise aggregate demand and generate new business possibilities.

6. Enhanced Corporate Governance and Risk Management: Strengthening corporate governance norms and supporting effective risk management techniques can help prevent firm failures and enhance resilience to economic shocks. This involves fostering transparency, accountability, and ethical corporate practices, as well as strengthening risk assessment and mitigation capacities inside firms.

Calls for Structural Changes to Enhance Economic Stability

In addition to short-term policy adjustments, there are rising calls for structural improvements to boost the long-term stability and resilience of the Russian economy. These structural changes attempt to address underlying shortcomings and vulnerabilities that contribute to economic instability and intensify the impact of exogenous shocks.

1. Diversification of the Economy: Accelerating efforts to diversify the economy away from overreliance on natural resources, particularly oil and gas, is vital to decreasing susceptibility to commodity price changes and external shocks. This entails fostering growth in non-resource industries such as manufacturing, technology, and services through targeted investments, innovative incentives, and regulatory changes.

2. Investment in Human Capital and Innovation: Investing in education, skills development, and research and development (R&D) is crucial to promoting a more dynamic and competitive economy. This involves expanding financing for education and vocational training programs, rewarding R&D investment through tax credits and grants, and fostering collaboration between academics, business, and government to stimulate innovation and entrepreneurship.

3. Improvement of Infrastructure and Logistics: Enhancing infrastructure and logistics networks is vital to boost connectivity, decrease transportation costs, and enhance competitiveness. This involves investing in transportation infrastructure, improving logistical hubs and ports, and modernizing digital infrastructure to support seamless trade and investment flows.

4. Protecting the Rule of Law and Institutions: Upholding the rule of law, protecting property rights, and promoting judicial independence are necessary to boost investor confidence, preserve property rights, and provide fair and efficient dispute resolution. This includes modernizing legal and regulatory frameworks, eliminating corruption, and boosting institutional ability to enforce contracts and defend investors' interests.

5. Fostering Small and Medium-Sized Enterprises (SMEs): Supporting the growth and development of SMEs is vital to stimulating entrepreneurship, innovation, and job creation. This involves providing tailored assistance programs for SMEs, enhancing access to capital and markets, decreasing regulatory barriers, and fostering entrepreneurial education and training.

6. Integration into Global Markets: Deepening integration into global markets and boosting international trade and investment may increase competitiveness, encourage technology transfer, and enable economic growth. This comprises pushing trade liberalization, strengthening trade agreements, and boosting the business climate to attract foreign investment and encourage export-oriented growth.

In conclusion, tackling the corporate bankruptcy spike and fostering economic stability in Russia require a holistic approach that blends short-term legislative improvements with long-term structural changes. By executing targeted policy interventions and embracing structural changes, Russia can manage the current crisis, create resilience, and establish the framework for sustained economic growth and prosperity in the future.

Chapter 11

International Perspectives and Collaborative Efforts

In today's linked global economy, knowing foreign perspectives on corporate bankruptcies is vital for appreciating the larger consequences and finding potential joint initiatives to address the issue. This chapter dives into ideas from worldwide views on corporate bankruptcies, analyzes prospects for international cooperation, and helps in solving this complicated topic.

Insights from Global Perspectives on Corporate Bankruptcies

Corporate bankruptcies are not unique to Russia; they occur globally and are driven by a range of factors, including economic conditions, legal frameworks, and market dynamics. By analyzing experiences and insights from different nations, we can obtain useful perspectives on the causes, effects, and management of corporate insolvency.

One noteworthy example is the United States, where corporate bankruptcies are managed by Chapter 11 of the Bankruptcy Code. Insights from the U.S. experience underscore the relevance of restructuring tools, creditor rights, and court monitoring in allowing orderly reorganizations and maintaining value for stakeholders. Similarly, European nations provide varied methods for corporate bankruptcy, ranging from formal court-driven proceedings to informal out-of-court exercises.

Moreover, rising economies such as Brazil, India, and China have encountered their own troubles with corporate bankruptcies, typically contending with issues of creditor protection, judicial efficiency, and access to funding. By comparing the experiences of different nations, we may discover common patterns, best practices, and new ideas that may be applicable to the Russian environment.

International institutions such as the International Monetary Fund (IMF), the World Bank, and the Organisation for Economic Co-operation and Development (OECD) also contribute essential research, policy suggestions, and technical support on corporate bankruptcy concerns. Drawing on their experience and resources, we can expand our awareness of global patterns of business bankruptcy and inform policy discussions and reform efforts in Russia.

Opportunities for International Cooperation and Support

In the face of growing business bankruptcies, possibilities for international collaboration and support exist, affording channels for exchanging expertise, resources, and best practices to boost Russia's capacity to confront the issue effectively.

One area of partnership lies in capacity building and technical support. International organizations and donor agencies can provide training programs, workshops, and consulting services to increase the skills and competence of Russian policymakers, regulators, and practitioners in the field of corporate bankruptcy. By boosting institutional capacities and fostering good governance practices, such measures can contribute to a more strong and resilient bankruptcy framework in Russia.

Furthermore, cross-border collaboration across countries can ease the resolution of international insolvencies and the recovery of assets for creditors. Mechanisms such as the UNCITRAL Model Law on Cross-Border Bankruptcy provide a legal framework for coordinating bankruptcy procedures involving corporations with activities or assets in different countries. Strengthening collaboration procedures and fostering reciprocal acceptance of international proceedings can speed the settlement process and lessen the danger of asset dissipation in cross-border cases.

Additionally, international forums and networks offer opportunities for conversation, information sharing, and policy coordination among stakeholders from different nations. Participating in conferences, seminars, and working groups allows Russian authorities and practitioners to connect with their counterparts from across the globe, share experiences, and learn from global best practices. These meetings build a collaborative atmosphere and cultivate a shared awareness of the difficulties and opportunities in handling business bankruptcies on a global scale.

In conclusion, utilizing ideas from global perspectives and embracing chances for international collaboration and support are key steps in confronting the spike in company bankruptcies in Russia. By tapping into the collective experience and resources of the international community, Russia can increase its resilience, stimulate innovation, and develop a more sustainable framework for corporate insolvency resolution in the years ahead.

Chapter 12

Future Outlook and Emerging Trends

Predictions on the Future Trajectory of Russia's Economy

As we look ahead, estimating the direction of Russia's economy means navigating through a complicated web of geopolitical, economic, and social elements. While the nation has proven resilience in the face of multiple obstacles, including sanctions and international tensions, uncertainties loom large, defining the future picture. Here, we look into expert analysis and projections to shed light on what lies ahead for Russia's economic environment.

1. Geopolitical Dynamics: The geopolitical situation will continue to play a crucial role in influencing Russia's economic trajectory. Ongoing tensions with Western nations, particularly related crises in Ukraine and Syria, as well as differences over energy policy and human rights concerns, will undoubtedly impact the course of economic policies and foreign relations. Experts predict that diplomatic measures to alleviate tensions may bring some relief, but the persistence of geopolitical concerns remains a critical issue.

2. Energy Markets and Oil Prices: Russia's economy remains strongly reliant on energy exports, notably oil and gas. The future trajectory of global energy markets, including variations in oil prices and moves towards renewable energy sources, will greatly affect Russia's economic prospects. Analysts expect that diversification initiatives and investments in renewable energy infrastructure may provide some resilience against volatility in traditional energy markets. However, issues in responding to a fast-developing energy market might offer considerable impediments to sustainable economic growth.

3. Sanctions and Economic Policies: The efficacy and length of international sanctions placed on Russia will continue to impact the country's economic outlook. While Russia has made attempts to reduce the impact of sanctions through import substitution programs and efforts to boost domestic sectors, extended restrictions may limit foreign investment, technical innovation, and access to global markets.

Analysts say that addressing sanctions-related issues would need adaptive economic strategies, diplomatic measures, and structural improvements to create resilience and limit negative repercussions.

4. Domestic problems and structural reforms: Internally, Russia has a multiplicity of economic problems, including structural inefficiencies, bureaucratic hurdles, and demographic upheavals. Addressing these concerns will be vital for sustaining long-term economic development and prosperity. Experts underline the need to undertake structural reforms to improve the business climate, promote productivity, and stimulate innovation. Key areas for change include reducing regulations, raising investment in education and healthcare, and supporting entrepreneurship and small company development.

5. Global Economic Trends and External Dependencies: Russia's economic future is inextricably tied to larger global economic trends and developments. Shifts in international trade dynamics, technological breakthroughs, and geopolitical realignments will have rippling impacts on Russia's economy. Analysts underline the necessity of diversifying trade connections, minimizing dependence on unpredictable markets, and tapping potential given by rising economic trends such as digitalization and sustainable development.

In summary, while Russia's economy faces several obstacles and uncertainties, there are also prospects for development and resilience. Navigating the intricate mix of global factors, economic policies, and internal changes will be important for charting a sustainable path ahead. By utilizing its strengths, fixing shortcomings, and adjusting to emerging global trends, Russia may position itself for greater economic stability and prosperity in the years to come.

Identifying Emerging Trends and Potential Developments

Amidst the dynamic landscape of Russia's economy, various rising trends and possible events are set to impact the nation's trajectory in the future. These trends represent both difficulties and opportunities, bringing insights into areas of development, innovation, and transformation. Here, we discuss significant developing trends and their importance for Russia's economic future.

1. Digital Transformation and Innovation: The digitization of industries and the adoption of cutting-edge technology are driving transformational shifts across sectors. In Russia, the government has prioritized digitization activities as part of wider modernization plans. Emerging trends include the growth of digital infrastructure, the expansion of e-commerce platforms, and the integration of sophisticated technologies such as artificial intelligence and blockchain. These developments are projected to boost efficiency, productivity, and competitiveness, while also offering new opportunities for entrepreneurship and innovation.

2. Green Economy and Sustainable Development: The worldwide trend towards sustainable development and environmental conservation is gathering steam, bringing both difficulties and possibilities for Russia. As the globe advances towards renewable energy sources and low-carbon technology, Russia faces pressure to lessen its reliance on fossil fuels and address environmental concerns. Emerging trends include investments in renewable energy projects, acceptance of green technology, and measures to encourage sustainable development practices. Embracing the green economy may not only alleviate environmental hazards but also stimulate economic development, job creation, and technological innovation.

3. Shifts in Consumer Behavior and Market Dynamics: Changing consumer tastes and behaviors are redefining market dynamics and demand patterns. In Russia, expanding urbanization, rising wages, and shifting demographics are driving changes in consumer tastes, leading to greater demand for convenience, quality, and tailored products and services. Emerging trends include the expansion of digital platforms, the growth of e-commerce and online shopping, and the desire for sustainable and ethically sourced items. Understanding and reacting to these trends will be vital for organizations to remain competitive and relevant in a quickly developing market context.

4. Globalization and International Integration: Despite geopolitical tensions and trade limitations, Russia remains interwoven into the global economy, bringing both possibilities and problems. Emerging trends include the increase of international trade relationships, diversification of export markets, and participation in global value chains. Russia's strategic location, plentiful natural resources, and qualified people position it as a vital player in regional and global markets. However, geopolitical uncertainty and trade obstacles pose hazards to international integration, necessitating adaptive policies and diplomatic endeavors to negotiate complicated geopolitical dynamics.

5. Demographic Changes and Labor Market Dynamics: Demographic trends, including aging populations and shifting workforce dynamics, are transforming labor markets and economic landscapes. In Russia, falling birth rates, emigration, and an aging population pose problems for labor force participation and production. Emerging themes include efforts to address demographic concerns through immigration policy, investments in education and healthcare, and programs to boost workforce participation and skill development. Harnessing the potential of human capital will be vital for driving economic development, innovation, and social change in Russia.

In summary, emerging patterns and probable changes give significant insights into the future trajectory of Russia's economy. By embracing innovation, sustainability, and international collaboration, Russia can manage problems and grab opportunities to build inclusive growth, prosperity, and resilience in the years ahead.

This chapter presents a detailed examination of the future outlook and developing trends in Russia's economy, focusing on expert perspectives and research results. Through a sophisticated grasp of geopolitical dynamics, economic policies, and societal developments, stakeholders may better predict and respond to problems and opportunities, steering the nation towards a path of sustainable growth and prosperity.

Conclusion

Summary of Key Findings and Insights

In researching the spike in business bankruptcies in Russia, numerous major facts and insights have emerged, offering light on the underlying dynamics and repercussions of this crisis.

Firstly, the dramatic increase in company bankruptcies in Russia, notably in the first two months of 2024, indicates the confluence of several economic, geopolitical, and regulatory variables. These include the lingering impacts of the COVID-19 epidemic, sanctions imposed by Western countries following Russia's invasion of Ukraine, and internal issues such as high interest rates and financial instability.

Secondly, while some may link the surge in bankruptcies to the expiration of moratoriums established during the epidemic and sanctions era, it is apparent that underlying structural weaknesses within the Russian economy have also played a significant role. These include inefficiencies in the legal and administrative framework regulating bankruptcy processes, limited access to funding for firms, and a lack of adequate support channels for failing organizations.

Thirdly, the repercussions of company bankruptcy transcend the economic world, influencing the broader economy and society. Job losses, interruptions to supply chains, and lower investor confidence are among the bad results, further worsening economic issues and social tensions inside the country.

Moreover, the reaction to the crisis has been uneven, with government initiatives such as proposed tax hikes and modifications to bankruptcy rules meeting resistance and mistrust from numerous groups. There is an obvious need for more coordinated and effective initiatives to address the core causes of the bankruptcy rise and reduce its harmful consequences for the Russian economy.

Overall, the spike in company bankruptcies in Russia highlights the need for addressing chronic economic weaknesses and enacting comprehensive reforms to foster sustainable growth, resilience, and stability.

A Call to Action for Stakeholders to Address the Crisis

Addressing the epidemic of corporate bankruptcies in Russia needs comprehensive efforts from all parties, including government agencies, enterprises, financial institutions, civil society groups, and foreign partners. The following activities are advocated to successfully solve the difficulties at hand:

1. Policy changes: Government authorities must prioritize substantial changes aimed at correcting the fundamental flaws in the legal and regulatory framework regulating bankruptcy procedures. This involves expediting bankruptcy proceedings, protecting creditor rights, and providing access to alternative dispute resolution systems.

2. Financial Support Mechanisms: Financial institutions and development agencies should collaborate to offer targeted financial support to struggling enterprises, including access to credit, debt restructuring help, and investment incentives. Such steps can help ease immediate financial stress and promote the revival of viable firms.

3. Capacity Building and Education: Efforts should be made to increase the capacity of enterprises, legal professionals, and government officials participating in bankruptcy proceedings through training programs, workshops, and knowledge-sharing efforts. This can increase the efficiency and efficacy of bankruptcy proceedings and encourage greater openness and accountability.

4. Stakeholder Engagement and Dialogue: Dialogue and collaboration among stakeholders are vital for identifying and implementing sustainable solutions to the situation. This involves working with business organizations, trade unions, consumer advocacy groups, and other stakeholders to ensure that varied viewpoints and interests are taken into consideration in decision-making processes.

5. International Cooperation: Given the global character of the economy, international cooperation and collaboration are vital for tackling the difficulties of company bankruptcies in Russia. Governments, multilateral organizations, and bilateral partners should work together to enable information exchange, technical assistance, and capacity-building measures targeted at improving economic stability and resilience.

6. Long-Term Economic Planning: Finally, stakeholders must adopt a long-term perspective in addressing the crisis, recognizing that sustainable economic development requires strategic planning, investment in human capital and infrastructure, and a commitment to inclusive growth and social development.

By implementing these initiatives, stakeholders can work together to alleviate the immediate repercussions of the rise of corporate bankruptcy in Russia and create the framework for a more resilient, inclusive, and successful economic future.

www.ingramcontent.com/pod-product-compliance
Lightning Source LLC
Chambersburg PA
CBHW071059240526
45471CB00016B/2172